The Banished and the Dead

Poems By

Anne Leigh Parrish

Unsolicited Press
Portland, Oregon
www.unsolicitedpress.com
info@unsolicitedpress.com
619–354–8005

THE BANISHED AND THE DEAD
Copyright © 2026 Anne Leigh Parrish
All Rights Reserved.
Printed in the United States of America.
First Edition.
ISBN: 978-1-963115-64-2

No part of this book may be used or reproduced in any manner whatsoever without written permission except in the case of brief quotations embodied in critical articles or reviews.

This is a book of poetry. The people, places, and events described herein are either entirely fictional, grossly exaggerated, or so bizarrely true that you'd never believe me anyway. Any resemblance to actual persons (living, dead, or undead) is coincidental—unless they recognize themselves, in which case… yikes. All rights reserved, even the ones you didn't know existed.

Distributed by Asterism Books
https://asterismbooks.com/

For wholesale orders:
Asterism Books
568 1st Avenue South, Ste 120
Seattle, WA 98104
(206) 485-4829
info@asterismbooks.com

Cover Design: Kathryn Gerhardt
Editor: Summer Stewart

To John, Bob, Lauren, Lacey, Sam, Frida, and Tsuga

Acknowledgments

"Another Day" appeared in *Feminine Collective*

"At My Mother's Knee" appeared in *Feminine Collective*

"Even the Desert" appeared in *Unleash Lit*

"History" appeared in *Unleash Lit*

"I'll Teach You" appeared in *Feminine Collective*

"Might" appeared in *Quartet*

"Our Mothers" appeared in *Tap Into Poetry*

"Perhaps" appeared in *The Bluebird Word*

"Poppy" appeared in *Feminine Collective*

"Strife" appeared in *Unleash Lit*

"The Fallen Down Forest" appeared in *Feminine Collective*

"The Silence It Accepts" appeared in *Unleash Lit*

"The Suburbanites Visit a Nightclub" appeared in *Unleash Lit*

"This Is the Year" appeared in *Literary Heist*

"Today's Sermon" appeared in *Feminine Collective*

"Waiting to Be Born" appeared in *Feminine Collective*

Contents

The Suburbanites Visit a Nightclub	13
The Silence It Accepts	14
Strife	15
History	16
Even the Desert	17
Perhaps	19
Sit Here with Me	20
Floating Bridge	21
July	23
We Serve Nothing	24
Poppy	26
Daring and Determined	28
Another Day	29
The Fallen Down Forest	30
Bouquet Behavior	31
Almost April	32
What If?	33
A Prayer for the Upper Sonoran	34
Take No Refuge	35
A Pearl, Perhaps	36
Can't We Call It Good?	38
I'll Teach You	39
Another War	40

Waiting to Be Born	41
Today's Sermon	43
Blue Baby	44
Hers to Make	46
Ode to the Common Bone	48
Accidental Life	50
Jean	51
The Banished and the Dead	53
As We All Are	55
Oak Hill Place	56
Dysfunctional Relationship	58
Now, Later	59
Forever	60
A Visit to the Old Neighborhood	61
The Gambler's Thrill	63
Maybe It Started Then	64
Summation	65
Bound	66
Hitch	67
Major Bling	70
Vintage Jewelry	71
No Name Given to What Is Lost	72
Handprint on the Wall	73
Those Snowfalls of Our Troubled Youth	74
Dreaming of Paris	75

Just by Wanting	78
Sisterhood Monetary Policy	80
A Sort of Melding	81
An Earlier Day	83
Mistaken Identity	84
Trove	85
All that Remains	87
Your Nothingness	88
Fuller Days	89
Dad, Laid Up	90
At My Mother's Knee	92
Our Mothers	93
Sorry, Mom	96
Interface	98
Whole	99
Liar	101
Many Stones	102
Indifferent to the Blood	103
He Waits	104
Fate	105
Tandem	107
Too Lightly	108
This Is the Year	109
Another Confession	110
Seasonal	111

Joy	112
A Recipe for Happiness	113
Never Tire	115
The Only One	116
Homeless in Missoula	117
False Haven	119
Rise	120
Lineage	121
What It's Not	122
Declined	123
Might	124
Scribe of the Domesday Book	125
Hey, Girl (Dedicated to Rembrandt van Rijn)	126
The Unworthy	127
This Dream	128

The Banished and the Dead

The Suburbanites Visit a Nightclub

The girl dances in the center of the room and
        in the corner you freeze

She's just dancing, I say
        But why must she do it here, where I can see?

Ignore her, I say
        Can I ignore a fire?

The girl dances on, drunk, ecstatic, her joy
        running its course like a fever

Drinks are served,
        we don't touch them

The girl twirls her last twirl and a laughing man
        leads her back to their own corner

I'm fire, I tell you, but
        you're on your phone now, tapping away

You don't know you're about to burn

The Silence It Accepts

Betrayal is the broken promise you never meant to keep

> (If you follow your own lights, and not those I assign you,
> Do you betray me?)

> (Was my assignment the betrayal?)

Betrayal is willful blindness, dismissal, ignoring one's humanity

Betrayal might be nothing more than failing to
Grant you dignity

To allow it, even

To hear it speak

Betrayal is deafness and the silence it accepts

Strife

Paint-by-number sky hangs over the city at night
Represents all places,
Everywhere
Summarized

Light takes so long to reach us
When we see it, it's all gone

Does starlight dim as it burns across space?

What I say today
Stings less over time

How young we were caused our strife
And all the bad stuff later

I'm sorry

If I pour life down the drain,
What's left in the trap?

You

History

Witty zingers
        arguments won
                shame accepted

A mountain
        on which to stand
                and name the rocks below

We forget what they're called
        I'm as guilty as you,
                my transgressions just as cruel

The mountain wears away
        to a grassy plain where we
                lie, ready to help each other back up

Even the Desert

When someone you love hates you,
You work so hard to bring them around

Water the brown plant
Floss your teeth
Get on the scale

No sweetness comes

To compromise is to lose ground

Hate is the hard surface, softened by the light-seeker
The brick wall clutched by a dark green vine

In the east, there are a lot of buildings like that
And the wet, damp smell of things lifting from the earth

In the west, water is scarce, thus cherished

No, I'm not sand, nor are you rain
We're just mismatched
Yet, even the desert blooms

Perhaps

We map disaster
Perilous seaways
Treacherous mountain passes
Forbidding terrains of all kinds

Do we hold it in common, or
Is there one map for you, and another for me?

We find ourselves on a tiny plot of land
In a strangely calm sea

How do we escape?
The map is blank
Faded and burned by the sun

We'll draw a new one, you say
With clear paths and gentle views
No, I say, that's a silly fantasy
You say, perhaps, but some call it faith

Sit Here with Me

Living by candlelight is lovely
Until wax hollows or wind
Shivers the flame

The glow is pleasant, draws one in
But don't come too close!

That enticing invitation,
Followed by a blazing touch
Can destroy

Like the love of some people

Don't think of that now, just
Sit here with me,
Close, but not too close

Floating Bridge

On one side of the bridge, the lake roils,
On the other side, all is calm
A clear case of opposites
Or the power of one thing to
Break the rolling sweep of another

I stand between you and disaster
Absorb the blows, keep out the rain
Not as elegant as that bridge
Not built by the hand of man
(Even yours)
Yet I'm a tough old broad, someone (with a
Weakness for film noir) once said

As a roof shelters, so does the heart
The trick is to seek it
And protect it, if you can

July

The top of summer
> isn't the hottest or longest day,

But the moment when nothing stirs, birds fall silent,
> even children cease their raucous glee

Could we tip back in time to when light was new?
> or forward to when it dims?

You fade as easily as mist
> rises from a morning lawn

Only your voice remains,
> tickling my ear with whispers I can't make out

You may return when wind lifts summer into fall,
> but you won't be welcome

Having learned the art of stillness,
> I've no use for the muddy swirl you call love

We Serve Nothing

All those dreams of rising from the ground
    that visit children at night

Gravity a lie, just another confection from some
    wig-wearing affluent man

Then there are the deep ancestral memories
    of falling from trees

Laugh and lie prone below heaven's dome
    hunger for the brilliance found there—

Light, clouds, birds,
    wit, the only weight

Comes the butterfly in the green-needled branch
    a first look brings fear, another, rage

What right has it to be glorious
    while we struggle to rule?

Name, classify, maybe pin it to a board,
    anything to make it ours

Beauty can't be owned,
    and we're fools to think it can

When we're gone and the planet
        spins more cooly

The butterfly will dazzle no one, just keep the flowers
        alive and well

Beauty serves beauty, one might say
        while we serve nothing but our own despair

Poppy

A single crimson poppy flutters in weedy grass,
      catches the light like blood

Wasn't that grand, we ask
      just there for us to find

You didn't mean to say like blood, did you?

The damaged ceiling comes down to
      reveal a beam singed by fire

What you can't see hides in silence
      with a ragged-clawed animal that

Lives on flesh, then sets the world alight

On its day off it might give the wind a seed
      to play with and drop at will

Hence, our shimmering poppy

On another day, we'll say it
      glows like that ruby stone in the ring I

Gave you back, saying I can't, not now
      maybe not ever

Daring and Determined

Love, or anger?

Which keeps those two soaring birds together
        as warm air lifts them from sun-soaked earth?

This is the big empty of Central Washington
        where one forest is behind, and the next hours away

Anger and love reside in every tumbleweed and stalk of grass,
        though not in equal measure

Which prevails, and why?

Ask the birds, as they dart, swoop, and
        keep a daring, determined focus, one upon the other

Another Day

Light rises around the sheltering house
Weaves reality from dreams
Draws breath from bruised lips
Nudges us into the familiar
Another day!
Anything is possible, if not probable
Water boils, coffee
Brews, bread
Browns, butter
Goes bad, milk
Sours, paper's late again
Our resolve to continue
Mimics the worm's drive to
Wriggle through wet earth until a beak
Snatches it away
No beak for us
We've already been taken
Already surrendered

The Fallen Down Forest

Leaves go
Sightlines clear
This is winter's remark

Leaning trees
Crazy cross-hatch, we
Rail against each other

Now things are laid bare and
Propped up
Out of love's long habit

The strife will quiet as darkness
Bears down
Leave it until spring, the trees will
Hide their torn ground, too

Bouquet Behavior

Some arrive reluctant to open,
        give nothing for a day, two, three

Then, as if tiring of their
        self-imposed reticence, sing

Heady scent and fierce beauty reposition us against
        disappointment and failure

Some bring promise in their closed heads, great ideas take shape
        petals hold together, dark secrets never told

We come around to their silence and stillborn state
        find richness in it, a touch of wisdom, too

Almost April

Ha, ha, says the rising light
    you didn't think I'd make it

Cold, wet dark lasts so long with
    no time off, the

Blind rock spins, tilts, shoves its plates an inch here,
    a mile there, pretty much routine by now

And you, all the while stand in a trap of your
    own making, or locked in by another's hand

You're given darkness
    and now comes your reprieve!

A reminder to have faith, not in what
    you wish for, but in what you see with

Your own eyes, record dutifully in the fabric of your memory,
    bet money on, if you're the gambling kind

Light swings back around to tease dark
    and says, ha, ha, you're not the only game in town

What If?

Drift over the landfill
Take it all in
Like a collage, isn't it?
Clothing, a patchwork quilt
Empty soda bottles a lovely green

To see beauty in ugliness
Means there's hope

But for what?
To accept the harm we do? Ignore it, even?

No celebration there, just a study in denial

Might we look closely at everything, all the time and
Ask, what if?

A Prayer for the Upper Sonoran

White sky, saguaro thin and brown,
Hollowed by thirst,
Yet the desert delights,
Feeds my hunger for escape

I beg the wind to carry me
To a point of no return
More than a lifetime away

Take No Refuge

Maps change, but from space
        earth looks the same

Soon there will be less forest,
        more blue ocean

My home rearranges itself, my visitors are redrawn,
        Kip is wise, Jean so sweet, Steve is never gone

Are dreams the only constant,
        and truth what melts away?

Take no refuge in sleep
        we have too much work to do

A Pearl, Perhaps

Religion's clutch comes from stories we
Pen and name

We are the miracle in the universe, yet fable-makers
Need something more

We're too hard to take at face value
Our existence impossible without design
Our ability to reason handed down

We are made small, flawed, corrupt so we may be
Corrected, punished, improved

Needing a script to follow is just a power grab, right?
All the Holier-than-Thou men can't wait to
Burn us down

Can't We Call It Good?

You can argue that we created god to rejoice in the miracle of life, but I think it was to keep us safe from fear and loneliness here on this rock, with nothing but freezing black space all around. Of course, we took a while to figure out that's where we were. We used to think we were the center of everything, that it all revolved around us—such narcissists. Maybe that was the original sin. Isn't ignorance always arrogant? Then there's the animal within to contend with, the one urging us to murder and maim, no good if you want to get along with your neighbors. But is an imaginary friend really the way? Not that god is so friendly. Lots of vengeance there, all that smiting and plagues of locusts. Why can't we look at conscience and call it good? Do we need a paternal figure looking over our shoulder? Someone to wave a magic wand and make everything right? Depends on how sad, scared, or sick we are, and how much pain we have to give away.

I'll Teach You

Sorrow sings to men who sleep with guns
Time erodes land to dust and bodies to bone
Sky loses color, rivers run black

How can masculinity survive?
Who says it has to?

My ovaries are not your mistress
My hands are not your maid
If you want to preach natural law I'll
Teach you about mitochondrial DNA

Another War

When men lose their balance, they blacken the blooming field
Cool heads do not prevail, water
Wears down stone, but what
Ends violence, when each man
Wants his share?
Even in the game of fantasy chess, a pawn can
Take a king, rain
Ends drought, then becomes a flood

Waiting to Be Born

On a blank wall a purple line rises and falls as the painter walks alone, can in hand, heart fast, breath shallow, hopes high. The line will soon disappear at the hand of another painter, hired to cover this expression of joy, as it will be thought of by the painter/eraser, deciding, based on the color alone that the joy is female. His mother loved purple; hence the can of purple paint was held by a woman, or a womxn, a word he can't pronounce but which is seen on many walls here, in this liberal forest town. Some people change their gender, say they're trapped in the wrong body, which must suck, thinks the eraser/painter, applying his brush. Some women wish to become men, but more often it's men who yearn to cast off their maleness and become women, like that guy on that show with the rich family in California. His mother says to accept god's will, but the painter/eraser doesn't believe in god. He just finds it weird that someone would hate being a man given all the crap women go through, not to mention being second-class citizens, a concept his wife has pushed his way for years until he just says yeah, I hear you, honey, though in truth things aren't too great for guys, either, witness the fact that here he stands, in a lousy job, one that's never going to make his dreams come true. What were they, those dreams? To be himself, to find his gifts, to paint lines on a wall, like the purple woman. How he envies her! The woman has no envy, only this can in her hand, the paint she sprays, the sidewalk she's on alone, the night around her soft and quiet, like a spirit waiting to be born.

Today's Sermon

Hold still while I rape you
Set you on fire
Slap you down

Don't move
Or dream
No starlight for you

Receive me whenever I must
Relieve my rage and lust

Your body belongs to me
And your soul belongs to god

You own nothing
Not even the dirt on which you lie,
Weeping

Blue Baby

You're my out-of-the-blue baby, and
    oh baby, do you make me blue

No doubt about it, baby,
    blue equals me plus you

Wish I saw you coming, I'd have run the other way
    forever and a day just to say . . .

Steer clear, baby, and let my blue heart heal

Next time you see me, that old thing
    will be made of steel

Hers to Make

Light shines on her auburn locks from the sidewalk to the dock,
    tick-tock of life's clock

Sun in her eyes gives him the lie
    how she gets by

A nursery trick to sound sweet and gentle
    simple, even mental, then pull a fast one

Her head came off, said the arrogant toff, and I rolled it down the lane,
    before too long, to accompany my song, it reduced itself to brain

But, back to this woman on the dock—

Striding toward the place where one life ends,
    and another begins

Perhaps there will be a boat with a leaky outboard motor
    leaving a trail of gasoline to glisten in the sun and

Remind her of something beautiful and proportionate
    and is anything but

Will she mind it when she finds it?
    Regret what another beget?

No

As long as she's shown respect and
>	her choices are hers to make

Ode to the Common Bone

A bone to pick suggests we might dine together
And find a wishbone?
Who would pull the larger share?
Just where would that bone snap?

If you eat me down to the bone, I will end
Your starvation and you will
End my life

Winter leaves us hungry for warmth
When sun returns, our bones
Lie naked and bleached

The bird stays aloft because its bones are hollow
Our marrow isn't all that keeps us grounded
Grief is weightier than flesh, and never ages

Femur neck risks a fracture
Bones like a brittle sponge
A tooth for every child

Boneyard waits
Dust pile grows
Carried off by wind

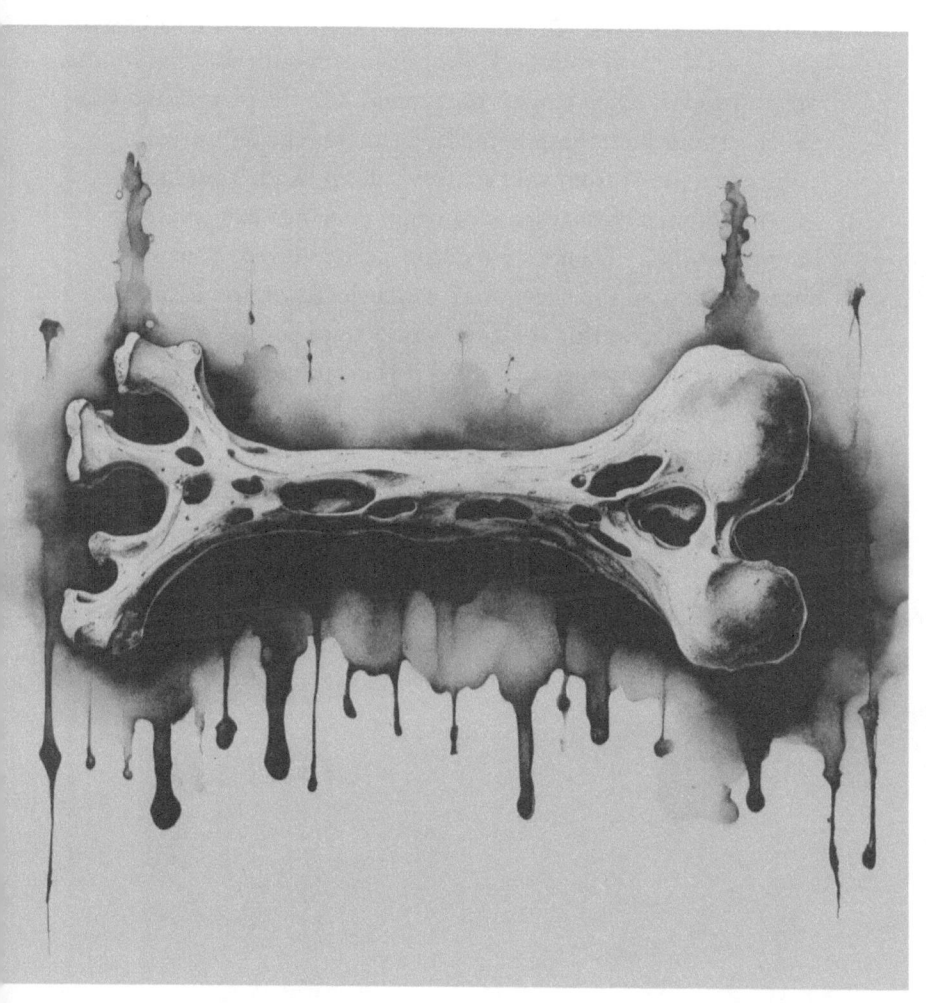

Accidental Life

Summer camp trail ride, once again you're at the end of the line. Pony canters to keep up, tosses you in a flash, sky bears witness to you down there on your back, dust in your mouth, gasping for the breath you lost when you hit the ground. On the playground you fall, gash your knee, limp home late, receive rebukes for your tardiness, a pinch from your mother's sharp hand. Your father leaves without a word, then on a whim demands your presence, his girlfriend too drunk to stand, his speech slurred. Your sister abandons you on the street of a small Swiss town, round and round you go, covering the same blocks until you ask a shopkeeper in your broken French if you can use his phone. He dials your grandfather's apartment, soon your mother and sister arrive, enraged that you wandered off. All of them dead now, yet live on in you with a fire time can't put out. Once lit, you burn forever.

Jean

Dinner parties are Jean's thing, the carrot she chases, beaten by the stick of failure. Terrified of being shunned. Not an independent spirit, in other words. A free thinker only when expressing cruelty. She slaps down the chicken breasts, pounds dough, rips lettuce leaves to shreds. Next to cooking, seething is her talent, that silent, steely rage. I'm not allowed in the kitchen unless ordered there. Childhood = indentured servitude.

Once they swirl in, all perfume and cigarette smoke, she's smiles and grace. So witty, so kind.

She despises them, the people she feeds, for being what she isn't— married and safe. Playing the plucky divorcée only goes so far when what you want is someone to take charge, be the parent, keep out the wind and rain.

~

The cards slap down hour after hour. A cigarette lodges in the corner of her dry mouth. Solitaire for the solitary seeking vengeance.

The deck is shuffled fifteen, twenty times, and if I ever dare touch those cards, I'll find them as soft as butter from the bending and flexing in her angry hands.

~

Later, in Paris with Jean's best friend, Jacqueline. Strong coffee and sympathy. Lots of cigarettes. At the table, covered with thick blue oilcloth, they sit by the hour, nattering in French. I understand it all. *Bien sur!* Jean shares a dream. At the market she chooses a green cabbage to bring home and once there, removes the outer leaves, then more leaves until she reaches the center which is rotten and brown. Poor Bibette (Jean's nickname), Jacqueline says, *quelle horreur!* Whose heart has she peeled away? Mine? Hers? My absent father's? All our hearts are rotten now.

The Banished and the Dead

The operator reads the telegram word by word, letter by letter
It's in French and you know what it says
You didn't like him much, that Swiss grandfather
Sharpening his pencils with a knife
Fingers yellow from cigarette smoke
Had a jaunty stride, though
You can give him that
Your mother comes home, you
Go down, paper in hand, then outside to
Meet her by the car, and it
Occurs to you that she is stylishly
Dressed today in a sleeveless lavender dress
Is that a brooch near her shoulder?
And those square sunglasses are a gas
A quick pass over your neat blocky lettering and she
Says, *now I'm alone*
Husband with a new wife
Mother long dead
Now this old man out of her hair
And what of you?
Twelve years old and full of life
The cold shadow at her side

As We All Are

The older brother was the better toy, and all the girls knew it.
As the quietest, I was given the younger one to chase, but he
wouldn't be caught, wouldn't play the game, preferred to sit with
a book, smile dreamily as he turned each page, the story alive in
him the way nothing else was, certainly not me. Such splendid
independence, this gentle isolation, flesh and blood a concept.
Where is he now, the boy in the school uniform? The lives I
assign him all end badly—books shunned, blindness creeping, a
small apartment in a rough neighborhood; my own malaise to
blame. I've grown cruel with age. Why should I think ill of one
who preferred the page to me? Regret, I suppose, leads the heart
to yearn for a different past. We might have lived together, books
everywhere sitting by the fire at night, Mozart in the background,
rain on the pane, like-minded, traveling the same road. Even so,
I'd have been alone, as we all are, but it would have taken longer
to see with love and kindness to distract me.

Oak Hill Place

I stand in my kitchen today, right now
    and in another, long ago, as a child,
        my throat on fire, my cheek
    slapped by my mother's
Raging hand—

And in one that is part of a
    larger place, a building for people like
        me, who are frail, fuzzy in the head
        but still with it enough
    to turn off the stove
When the phone rings—

Oh, it's you, asking if I recall
    those days on Oak Hill Place
        before they remodeled the house—
I do, and wish to hell I didn't

Especially when Aunt Kip fell down
    the basement stairs thinking she was
        opening the bathroom door—
Drunken sot

Time follows a a wide ellipse that
    narrows around the single point

> where it's possible to stand
> and impossible to do anything
> but grieve our expulsion by those who

Cast us off

Dysfunctional Relationship

Always so confessional, the rare times we meet
        can't stop the data dump

My silly need to connect, to
        make you the mirror that reflects my best self

You weave my words into a stiff, narrow scarf,
        smother me, choke me, strangle me

You're determined to shut me up
        yet the scarf stays hidden

So, I'll keep yapping about all the aches and pains
        my heart suffers

All of them caused by you

Now, Later

Later, they died
Rocky streams
Grassland
You swear to return there one day
Lower, then lift the curtain
Yours are the only working hands now

More snow falls that can be quartered
Streets gone
Houses lost
Nothing but silence
Freezing
The universe has her way

Forever

You wait, count the minutes in a room that
        lies down with the dark
Alone
Blades dance
They left you again
Eight?
Nine?
She's there, somewhere,
        mad child with a witch's face
Time wears on, your death minutes away, and
        your rebirth, moment by moment
        at their cold, conniving hands

A Visit to the Old Neighborhood

What I didn't gather sits in houses
        overlooking bright water

Others did better, stronger hands,
        maybe sturdier hearts

Though facades hide all
        kinds of mayhem

That's why they're so pretty
        and well-tended—usually

Disappointment can be bitter,
        envy, mad

My pile of acorns stacks up just fine
        the joy of building it worth celebrating

The Gambler's Thrill

Tell me of your thieving days, the
ones and fives
        lifted from your mother's
wallet when she

Wails about hard times

A faceted yellow jewel, alone in a
drawer, no chain to hang on
        yours, too

Why this greed, this hunger?

Your emptiness dares you, yet
the gambler's thrill
        goes cold

No more filching, honest hands a
must

She accuses you of what you
didn't do,
        no reason to give her
cause to discover genuine fault

Maybe It Started Then

Paris peace talks fail, in the Louvre
> little men in gray tunics, (Red Chinese, my mother whispers)
> inspect crown jewels

This twelve-year-old doesn't care about the broken world,
> there's a party to attend, a pretty boy waits

Madame Ong runs a candle along my twisted hair,
> burning off the frizz and split ends

Her French is perfect, learned at school before she left Vietnam,
> her hands are milk, her eyes, the night sky

She envies me my American life,
> the big home she believes I have

I envy that whatever she found is better
> than what she lost

The reverse is true for me,
> my life will be spent searching

Summation

Before I could read or tie my shoes
I wandered empty rooms,
Wondered what silence meant

Where did everyone go?
If they weren't there, I wasn't, either
I didn't exist at all

But what was I, then?
A feature of their nightmare,
Or the summation of mine?

For years, they turned the light off and on
I wished for a candle to burn and
Snuff out at will

Children are forbidden matches,
Given the dishonor of neglect,
Handed death

Bound

Our rivers rushed, then diverged
Was it bound to happen?
Too good to be true, that we would
Remain close forever?
We might have, if not for that crazy boy
Interloper
Desperate, mad, wild in ways
We couldn't see
Until later
Love was knit, cast on, cast off
Somehow never fit
Yet we looked for it everywhere
Just not in each other

Hitch

You came out that way, right leg folded behind the left
No worries, until you got to your feet and ran, curls flying
Pigeon-toed little monster
But better than the Thalidomide babies
All your limbs present and accounted for

Your sister-witch sticks out her foot to trip you
Down you go
So many bruises
Scabs, weepy drops of blood
A new skin

Hitch in your stride
Witch on your back
Set the pigeons free, strengthen your gait
Stey by step you correct those little feet
(now size 9 ½)

The bad leg made a bad hip
The X-ray called out the lies you spun for years
>*It happened afterward*
>*Vitamin deficiency*
>*Something swam up from the gene pool*

Fact is, you descended from a
Twisted womb and can't walk right

Yet move fast
Mile after mile

Major Bling

To Boston we shall go! My mother set to flee, a friend's lavish home. Never clear where their money came from. A professor, former Resistance fighter, displayed his withered arm, ruined by a Nazi machine gun. Now they were galivanting, he and the new wife. It was the era of new wives. At thirteen, I was a predictable snoop. The master closet had drawers. Seriously. I'm not kidding. This was 1971 and California closets weren't a thing. This trophy wife had major bling, all lined up on velvet cloths. A pear-shaped diamond ring, fit my pinkie just right, so, I boosted it. Yup. They returned, thanked us so much for the house-sit, no mention made of that missing rock. Was it real? I scratched my mirror with it. They say diamond cuts glass. And it did. Fear moved in then, took right over, ran the show. Didn't want to get caught with the goods. So, I took it to a favorite place, the old golf course, with that stand of trees in the middle, like a little forest, and gave the ring a new home, maybe one day it was found, gasped and exclaimed over, or sank deeper into the earth, returning slowly to where it began, millions of years before.

Vintage Jewelry

The ring sat on another's finger decades before I could see, given by a man asking to marry or to be forgiven for his roaming heart. It held her gaze when all else was black. How terrible the world for a lonely, hell-bent woman, caught by a cruel, desperate man. Did he grow kinder? And she, harder? It's mine now, the ring, yellow diamond, sun on my aging hand.

No Name Given to What Is Lost

I was called a magpie, my dresser strewn with gum wrappers, barrettes, a newly minted nickel. How I hungered in those days for the immutable. The ring, an heirloom, thick, muddy red stone with strange lettering I later learned was Arabic. Your great-uncle's ring, they said. Forgotten until five decades later when I gave my spit to Ancestry.com. One percent of me derives from the Arabian Peninsula. How about that?

Handprint on the Wall

We were so dirty in those days, sweaty skin, oily hair
        too giddy and wild to mind

Your mother a purist,
        no handprints on her freshly painted wall

When I went away to Paris, got hauled off, to be exact
        my school, a mass of giggly tweens

Rode a train six hours south
        to the Lascaux caves

Low undulating ceiling, textured walls, bison maybe,
        game at least, sometimes a thrown spear

Correct proportions, serious intent
        a record of wonderment

And a handprint on the wall to say,
        Stop! Now go back the way you came

Those Snowfalls of Our Troubled Youth

Snow started in October,
    stopped

Landed hard in November,
    graced our strained, bleak holiday

Dragged us into a slushy New Year
    and when we thought foolishly of

The spring yet to come,
    WHAM

February blizzard
    too much snow even for Upstate

Cops on snowmobiles,
    classes cancelled

You, in your happy home two doors down,
    I, in a hamster wheel dodging darts

Cold is the calling card of the universe,
    its M.O.

Winter buried and insulated
    but never washed us clean

Dreaming of Paris

You can't find your passport, so you can't
      board the plane

Then, you're there, in a seat with a curved back,
      wrapped around you almost lovingly

You have no hotel room lined up,
      none can be found, so you call Jacqueline

Your mother's cousin,
      always kind, with a ready smile

Your fingers dial the number
      in the phone booth by magic

Isn't this all magic?

Her place is small and full of light,
      the couch becomes a bed

The curtain, a wall
      later, the streets are narrow

They twist, turn, you're lost but then
      find a wider sky

Where a bulging cathedral looks down
        this is it, the place you sought

What you know, come to know
        as you take in the carved stone faces

Some blind, the nose snapped off,
        one or both hands gone

Is that this is how we become the past
        and the past becomes us

Just by Wanting

My eyes so keen to find her I see her everywhere,
Yet my heart
Turns away
So many names I've called her, each one a wound
All old women wear her face, so I must, too
Legions of us, an army of the unredeemed
Wandering, in search of the sister who killed us
Just by wanting us dead

Sisterhood Monetary Policy

Buy, borrow

Shady deals
Receipts for services not rendered

Insults, my take-home pay

Your hatred grows with compound interest

—

You know the saying, *Not for love or money*

No love from you

—

Later, when pennies grow to dollars
A kind word, now and then
Greed belied,
Greed transcendent

—

Rage, the balloon payment
My debt for being born, a jumbo loan

A Sort of Melding

A clay tile guards the table from the hot dish
Hand-painted, blue, a kitten mangling a ball of yarn—
Gentle image with a touch of violence
You, serving lunch
All smiles now, but once the guests are gone,
You'll cut me open and ask me to bleed outside,
Off the carpet I vacuumed at your command—
Another look at the tile proves the kitten didn't capture the yarn
But is ensnared by it, almost joined, a sort of melding of the
      living
And the dead, or of the living and the not alive
You don't think I'm alive and can't feel pain
Just a block of wood to kick aside
Until the wood won't move, and it's you who breaks

An Earlier Day

You're never idle
There's always more misery to cause
Cruelty is the knife
Indifference, the blade

Antisocial personality disorder—
A fancy way of saying you
Can't feel anyone's pain

In an earlier day you'd have been
Whipped in the town square for
Being mad, or worse,

Burned for consorting
With the devil

Mistaken Identity

It's said that fog is ghostly,
        renders the world opaque

Softens and shifts an outline
        until we tire of trying to

Make sense of space without boundaries,
        and in frustration, look away

The solid world is necessary,
        a flight of fancy, not

You tongue is a claw,
        your hair flame

Hate without boundary flows
        like storm water to a drain

You're gone, dead, in a can underground
        and there's nothing soft or shifty about you

Doesn't sound like a ghost to me, that
        gives us this irritation and relief

Sorrow, perhaps, or grief
        alive in the blood, rooted in the bone

Trove

On a shelf sits a box, in the box letters
Lie, some by hand, most typed
Clackity clack, you think
A man in an office or tiny apartment, putting in another sheet
Checking the ribbon, catching her up on his day, week, month
Outlining a future she doesn't
Agree to, but doesn't reject

All she wants is to stab her father in the heart
Many hearts are stabbed before the blade dulls
A mésalliance, you think

A woman who wants to be alone shouldn't marry
A woman who lives on hate shouldn't bear a child
But here you are
Reading words pressed on the page eighty years ago

You put the letters back and wonder how to
Live with the sorrow you inherit

All that Remains

When the flesh goes and takes along the voice,
Eyes no longer bright
What's left?
Heirs nursing the hurts we
Caused, or giving thanks for the
Kindness we showed

Lessons learned

We're a box of letters, notebooks,
Recipes, a few campaign buttons if those
Mattered
Knick-knacks no one wants
That crazy hat

We're images in a photograph
Around which light bends

We're the light now
All that remains

Your Nothingness

My father sits in a warm room,
Overheated you might say,
Stuffy, even

The painting before him changes

Tel-u-vi-zhun

When you know someone is heading toward
The mind's rearrangement,
A not so gentle slaughter
What to do?

Accept easily that the
Indifference in his eye
Means he's lost who he was

He has himself, though
You're a blank to him
Make no impression,
Can't even spark the smallest thought
While his sharp-as-ever brain
Takes in your nothingness
Again

Fuller Days

When my hands become yours, I'll know
Same traits—the middle finger
Twists to the right

When your truth is mine, I'll grieve
And choose not to inherit you, yet
Your piano and desk are now mine

My hands hold the living and the dead
Yours clutch ash and my
Dreams of fuller days

Dad, Laid Up

Sometimes advice comes from
A man on his back, held there by a disk
Slipped while delivering the ball

I was there
Saw the whole thing
Thought he was doing a victory dance

So plebian, a bowling alley
So clichéd, his second wife taking away his bedpan

I'm a cliché, too, sitting there
My court-ordered custody visit
Fourteen and frantic for a future that won't be found
His useless second daughter

Where is Number One?
Off declaring her independence with mad antics
Love affairs
Motorcycles
Blue eye shadow and false lashes
Who's the cliché now?

Back to the advice from the prone pseudo-sage

Don't look so far ahead, he says
Shorten the telescope

Day by day is the best anyone can do
Ease your mind and calm your heart

From these words I take comfort, until
My mind grows wider than the sky and
My heart runs away with the spoon

At My Mother's Knee

Soap
Towels
Comb
Soft touch, then hard
Pinch
Pull
Draw blood
Love's full circle, fed by rage

I get it
You didn't want to marry him
Marry anyone

Some wear disappointment like a pearl choker with matching earrings
Some wear cruelty like a second skin
To torment is to liberate

Really?

You were lazy in yourself
Sorry later, I suppose

After you crippled me by stopping and starting the clock at your whim
Like a heart
That happened to be mine

Our Mothers

Their hands rest in laps, on skirts
Patterned with daisies and doves
Grip wooden spoons, peel off rubber gloves
When the dishes are done
Press silver tubes to lips
>*Pretty Peach*
>*Passion Pink*
>*Ravishing Red*

Their rings flash
Fluttering birds

Pearl necklaces lounge on silk scarves in dresser drawers
When I break the string, hail stones hit the floor

The blame you take shields me

Your punishment is harsh
It always is
When you call your little sister a bad name,
Your mouth is washed with soap

Your mother keeps you close, mine takes herself off

Now, they're both gone

Our daughters collect memories of us
Our hands are still

Sorry, Mom

Your eyes in my mirror, your smirk on my mouth
Clouds reflected in a puddle are calm,
An easy version of what's above

I'm a version of you
I'd rather be blind

I inherit your traits
Wear your pain
Repeat your sin

Interface

Through sunglasses at twilight, what
      hangs in the sky might be a filtered sun

The hour says no, it's the moon,
      looking exactly like the sun

Or what the sun looks like
      when it doesn't blind

Uncertainty wondrous

Walking down a mountain trail,
      spun out on two tabs of acid

Our feet meet earth in a jaunty rhythm that
      gathers me in a sparkle of cloth and reels me away

Am I here with you, descending, or
      lying in bed with you, dreaming?

Uncertainty horrible

The interface between what's real and what's not
      is the shadowy place where we begin and will surely end

whole

I reach for them like life rings, these men I want to love me. They will hold me up and keep the cruel sea from swallowing me. But they don't. They're stupid, these men, driven by their own crooked dreams and bent aspirations. Their hands push me under where light falls for a while then can't penetrate the darker depths. My hands are boneless and won't grasp. With no choice but to let go I sink and somehow rise again. The sea doesn't want me, either. When I learn to swim I need only the water's buoyancy, the waves rolling to the shore, bearing me along, and once there, I rise like the fabled Athena to say I've arrived, loveless perhaps, but whole.

Liar

Love is finite
Held in boxes and jars
More for her
Less for you

Build a life on lies and you either fall
Or believe

Luck is finite,
You quickly run out

Love is a house with room for one more,
Whose doors don't need handles or locks

The liar lives on, who knows
How vast her web?
To this day threads cling
Like sorrows never shared,
Never broken

Many Stones

Wait for light to fall and darkness to cloak
Time dinner to his arrival, tears to his departure
Listen for the telephone
Lean into silence that doesn't break

Forgive the dead, even if they don't deserve it
They can't wander the earth forever, can they?

Hold his hand, all roughness gone
Your river bears many stones and only some are smooth
Impatience won't round them faster,
But wears you down for good

Time chooses, you don't, yet you
Clutch what's given

Letting go is harder than hanging on

Indifferent to the Blood

Who will people this house, with its
Wide, pretty rooms?
Sunlight beckons but those at the window
Loving the view are nameless

Not dementia, just truth

Time can't be stopped

Gather, as we used to, back when I mattered
Sit on my knee, press your hand to mine
Soon, this overlap will break away and
Fling us where reckoning is hard,
Can't be guaranteed

The hallway narrows then gives way
Go from nothing to something
Gather light as it rises, falls
Or, burns slowly, like a longing decades old

Tear down the house brick by brick
The dead are indifferent to the blood
Day weeps into night

An empty house is kinder than an empty heart

He Waits

Icy air invites and she
Escapes, her face
Numbs, but not her heart, on and on
She walks

He waits by a window that
Looks into the yard where their dead son
Played, his heart
Screams, too, he can't
Tell her that, she can't
Hear him

Each leaving is a death
She might not return
She can only go so far on foot
What if she hitches a ride?
The driver falls in love with her and she with him?

No
Come on, now
Things like that don't happen

Only drunk drivers happen
And the ravages they leave behind

Fate

We are not yet dust
Dreams hold fast
Fingers brush crumbs from the table
A late winter sun warms the bones

Give better than you get
Though what you grasp is so much less
The tiniest part of us refutes the freezing
Black of space

What of the planets,
Rotating possibility?
Analogies aren't so simple
When you admit to clear complexity

We've nothing to pull against except our
Fate, written in the brilliant light of stars

Tandem

Pause for the season to rise and the hand to drop
Hope things move in tandem
Like the clock and sunlight
But sequence usually prevails
First fire, then ash
Wind, then the empty air it leaves behind
What survives is said to be strong
I say it's what death hasn't taken, yet
Grim outlook, I'm told
Okay, fine
You always had my best interests at heart
Even as you knocked me sideways
Hate filled the coffer until I
Buried it in the American West
Beauty bests a fiendish heart any day
Lower the hand and the season will rise

Too Lightly

We arrive an animal, tiny, loud, disastrous
To give the raw word and bawdy laugh
Rage so deep that even when you
Turn over a new leaf, start the next chapter,
Take the oath, shed your skin and touch up the eye shadow, it
Holds on, never eases
Tired, powerless against it, you carry it along
Until you feel that if it left you,
Leaving you free to love and rejoice,
You'd tread too lightly on the earth

This Is the Year

The morning lifts its yellow-white soul through the trees
Bathing the Douglas firs with light
Behind them the sky hangs in willful darkness,
Pulled by clouds needing to be on their way
Out there, over the water
Taking along a wish here, a hope there
This is the year my grieving will end
And rage will settle in the warming ground
A resolution not in my hands to shape
But not in anyone else's either
Sorrow is its own master
I, its subject
Time for a tiny rebellion,
Quick laughter, a stupid joke
Let it go, I say
Let me go with it

Another Confession

What are you without your ghosts?
Free?
Innocent?
Blessed?
The space within given to crimson and gold
Like Christmas, every day
And when ghosts
Give up the silence they
Swear to keep
Weep in your ear night by night
What to do?
Send them home
Beg for their quiet
Take the peace they grant until they
Rise again from dark freezing ground to
Tease another confession from your ragged heart
Another lie from your bitter mouth

Seasonal

The gull calls as it
Lifts from sodden ground
Not yet!
Rain on stone from the
Needle-choked gutter sings
Many more weeks to go
In violet morning light,
Twin buds pinned
Where the branch meets sky say
Soon!

Joy

Slips in unseen, hides in corners
Waits silently, like the seabed, where fallen bones
Rattle in the bellies of fish

We don't know what to call it, this thing that takes over
No need for worship or to fall on our knees
Grateful for it, sure
But let's not get carried away

How wary we are, how reluctant, yet we
Say we're owed and deserving now
After all this time and rivers of disappointment

So I ask, what kept you?

A Recipe for Happiness

The button hangs, ready to fall,
An able hand threads a needle

Control is false, skill is strength

Hearts wear out, patience frays
Where to sew love?

Follow beauty to her door
Become her, bring her forth

Recipe
Happiness

INGRIDIENTS

DIRECTIONS

Never Tire

The ocean thrums as waves
Meet the headland

Oval two-toned rock rests on sand
Drops of rain shine on a feather

After dark, bonfires
Stretch down the beach

Long ago, sentries lit their pyres to
Warn of the armada

Now, the only warning is that
Questions will go unanswered

We'll grow old, and never
Tire of the asking

The Only One

I pick up the phone to call you, then remember
You're dead

The house my friend lived in belongs to someone else
Invitations to the party have nowhere to go

I'm still here
Holding all of you in some changing
Part of me
Wishing we could gather
And forget who we were, or
Start again the frayed process of
Understanding

Drenched in summer light, we sit on the lawn
Sip lemonade and iced coffee,
Talk is gentle, kind

The mind's eye remakes what the heart knows
Yet what does truth matter now, when I'm the only one
It lives in?

Homeless in Missoula

Between the bike path and the
Clark Fork of the Snake River,
A tent is pitched

An off-kilter brain
Sparkles like sunlight on water

Here speak the villains
There stand the accused

Lovers who don't love enough
Truth that lies too much

Drag the river for your dreams
Silence your demons, if you can

If they won't give up their voice
Let them scream all they like

The river, choked with
Spring snowmelt, is louder
Than any pain of yours

Which is exactly why you came

False Haven

Life is made of stepping stones
Each a false haven in Fate's wild rush

Your mother, groped by her
Deviant father, stepped over
His perversion to
Land on a sharp, wobbly stone
Of suspicion and contempt

Your father, hollowed by fear
Joined up a week after Pearl Harbor,
Broke codes, got another gold bar on his sleeve
Only to find your mother's heart
Cold, and his next wife's soaked
In booze

Your river rages, too
Your stones turn beneath you
Yet, you balance beautifully
In the moment before you fall

Rise

Lift off
Rise on the plume of your unmet dreams
No need for fear
Birds do this all the time
See how their bright wings
Catch and turn the light
The higher you go, the less space you
Require of the earth below
This wider view puts you in context—
One of many
All standing, turning round and round
In their own lives
So many gorgeous moving parts
On this cobalt sphere
Now, descend, find solid ground,
Live in your own house
Keep your own counsel
Be a part of everything
Belong

Lineage

Know another's chain
Hear it rattle
Feel cold links in your hand
Lineage unites us
Keeps us close
Brings truth closer
Warm to it
Common humanity inescapable
Compassion, requisite
Indifference beckons death
Surrenders the key to the cell we're
Given to punish the callous heart

What It's Not

What is darkness but hunger for light?
Silence, but the need for sound?
Death is just the absence of life,
Yet nonexistence is impossible to fathom,
Once you know what it's like to wake up

What is forever except now writ large?
Hatred, but love turned cold?
But that's wrong, because when love
Goes, it leaves a dull blade—
Hatred is born of rage

And what begets that?
Loss of power, a diminished estate
If equity guarantees balance, injustice
Tips the scales

Now, age might be the disappearance of youth
A condition we can accept
If we see it as it is, rather than what it's not
Held in the mind, a photograph,
Some other gentle relic
We can celebrate life's work
With a touch of whimsy
And a slap of glee

Declined

The card was declined and he didn't have another
So he left his sub and split
Looked good, too
Thick slice of cheese, crisp lettuce, tomato, ham,
Generous smear of mayo

See, it was the image of him eyeing it,
Thinking how tasty it would be
That got me

I'd have paid
Made it a gift,
If the cashier's eye roll hadn't said
> *Loser*
> *Slacker*
> *Your own damn fault*
> *Bum*
> *Creep*
> *Beat it, pal, you're holding up the line*

A manager removed the abandoned sandwich
Said it couldn't be sold now

Wasted food, a hungry man with a maxed-out card
I, with useless regret

Might

In the store, held by fluorescent light and a squeaky cart
I thought I might fall
Hip down first, then shoulder
Then my mad, wild head

I'd like to lie on the scarred tile while folks
Rush and run
Someone's jacket a pillow
All eyes on me
Should I struggle to rise I would be denied
Begged to lie still

In the raftered ceiling
Roosts a trapped bird
Worn from seeking a way out

Its beady eye might meet my bleary one
As if to sing, *See how it is to fly no more*

Scribe of the Domesday Book

His pen drags ink across parchment
Candles flicker, wax drips upon stone floors
Keep me, keep me, beats his heart
Versed in Latin, given to god and Christ on the cross
His hand curls in pain, red lines the error
My fault, my fault, my grievous fault
This scraped, dried cowskin on which he
Records the worth of a fertile land,
Acre by acre, shire by shire,
Will be celebrated as high Medieval art
While his labor, the long, slow weight it
Is forgotten

Hey, Girl (Dedicated to Rembrandt van Rijn)

There she is in a cloth cap I call jaunty
But for her was everyday
Up there on the wall, meeting eye after eye

What impression do we make?
Traipsing in and out
Looking on, breathlessly

The light on her face has no source
How is that possible?
What are we being told?

Neither human nor divine
Just the thing we're drawn to,
Hold, and keep close

Until we grow too dim
To see or be seen,
And it remains, alone
For tomorrow's art lover
The desperately devoted

The Unworthy

Time erases
Buries
Floods, dries out
Steals names, land, livestock
We have no estate in time's field
Razed
Burned
Broken with the shaking fault
Our only currency, unwisely spent
Squandered on the unworthy
The Earth's core spins more slowly
While we are frenzied with grief
And hunger
Time will tell, they say
But Time is quiet
We forget how to listen

This Dream

What is this dream that lifts within and
        flows beyond my reach?

The plan to paint the barn
        lost out to August's heat

Weathered boards
        met the new year

Our resolutions fell away

Follow the stream to the bottomland
        where winter's chill eats bone

Spring's reluctance is vanquished
        by the light we give the dark

A woman weeps in the forest,
        then takes root

Sorrow is the ground we stand on

When it falls into the sea,
        we find only salt

About the Author

Anne Leigh Parrish's latest novel, *A Broken Window*, appeared in June 2025 from Unsolicited Press. *Diary of a False Assassin*, her latest poetry collection, arrived in December 2024, also from Unsolicited Press. Recent titles are *The Hedgerow*, a novel; *A Summer Morning*, a novel; and *If The Sky Won't Have Me*, a poetry collection. She is the author of eleven other books. She has recently ventured into the art of photography and lives in the South Sound Region of Washington State. Find her online at Facebook, Instagram, Threads, Blueksy, and Goodreads. Learn more about Anne at her website, www.anneleighparrish.com. Explore her photography at www.laviniastudios.com.

About the Press

Unsolicited Press is based out of Portland, Oregon and focuses on the works of the unsung and underrepresented. As a womxn-owned, all-volunteer small publisher that doesn't worry about profits as much as championing exceptional literature, we have the privilege of partnering with authors skirting the fringes of the lit world. We've worked with emerging and award-winning authors such as Amy Shimshon-Santo, Brook Bhagat, Elisa Carlsen, Tara Stillions Whitehead, and Anne Leigh Parrish.

Learn more at unsolicitedpress.com. Find us on Instagram, X, Facebook, Pinterest, Bsky, Threads, YouTube, and LinkedIn. Unsolicited Press also writes a snarky newsletter on Substack.

www.ingramcontent.com/pod-product-compliance
Lightning Source LLC
LaVergne TN
LVHW040104080526
838202LV00045B/3762